Snow Secrets

Lynn Levine

Heartwood Press
221 Partridge Road,
East Dummerston, VT
ISBN: 978-0-9703654-2-2

For information about permission to reproduce selections
from this book, write to
HEARTWOOD PRESS
221 PARTRIDGE ROAD
EAST DUMMERSTON, VT 05346

www.heartwoodpress.com
ISBN: 978-0-9703654-2-2

Dedicated to all those who helped me dance through

the forest again and, above all, Jane Erb,

Stephen Spitzer and my husband, Cliff Adler

Cover Designed and Illustrated by

Kristina Hickman

ACKNOWLEDGEMENTS

THANK YOU TO ALL who helped by giving critical feedback and support: Brook Levine-Adler, Carol and Michael Cohen, Tina Peters, Gordon Adler, Betsy Whittaker, Annamarie Pluhar, Cheryl Wilfong, Connie Woodberry, Fred Goldberg, Jill and Phoebe Green, Ruth Unsicker, Laura Evans, Sue Morse of "Keeping Track" and Tonia Wheeler.

Special thanks to Karen Hesse, Eileen Christelow, David Budbill, Benson Bobrick, Dede Cummings, and to my writing critique group, Monday's Child: Jessie Haas, Michael Daley, Andra Horton, Jeanne Walsh, John Gurney, Jay Callahan, Sarah Miller, Jo McNeill and Pam Becker.

Thanks also to my editors Bara MacNeill and Suzanne Kingsbury.

Snow Secrets

Chapter 1

Horse Jumping

With sparkling eyes and frosted eyelashes, Sarah rode Wind Walker from the corral to the barn. Sarah turned to look at Jasmine behind her. Jasmine was staring into the snow. Just as Sarah was about to look away, Jasmine yelled, "There's blood in Walker's tracks."

Sarah straightened up and pulled on Walker's reins, and he came to a stop.

Jasmine, short but strong, rushed toward Sarah with a face as red as the prints she was following. "What's wrong with you? Didn't you notice that Walker was limping? He must have scraped his leg on that wooden fence."

Walker, a rich dark brown quarter horse with a striking white stripe down his face, bit his sore leg and groaned.

Sarah pulled her boots out of the stirrups, swung her foot around, and jumped off.

"I didn't know. I'm sorry, Walker."

"That's the problem. You don't pay enough attention."

"What if I made it worse by riding him?"

Walker twitched as blood continued to ooze from a small cut on his right hind leg.

Sarah crossed her arms. "What should we do?"

"I've seen this before. I'll get the antiseptic. Rub him between his ears. You know—his sweet spot."

Once they were in Walker's stall, Sarah stroked the horse while she repeated, "You're going to be okay."

When Jasmine returned, she rubbed the antiseptic on Walker's leg. "Here's the scissor." Jasmine unrolled the dressing tape, which made a raspy sound. She wrapped the bandage around Walker's leg. "Cut the tape right where my finger is pointing. The cut looks worse than it is."

Once the bandage was in place, Jasmine unbuckled the saddle. Sarah tried to pull it off, but Jasmine said, "Let me do it."

With her nimble hands, Jasmine easily got the saddle off Walker and then placed it on the wall hooks.

Sarah took off her helmet and put it on one of the shelves. She would trade places with Jasmine anytime. Sarah might be smarter in school, but Jasmine understood horses.

Sarah brought a book into the barn and sat on one of the bales of hay just outside Walker's stall. After reading three chapters, she went to get something to eat. She opened the door to the arena, where she had left her backpack, and noticed the jumping bar was three feet off the ground.

If only she could soar so high. She could jump eighteen inches, two feet on a good day.

From the shadow in the corner of the room, Easy Girl, a Morgan horse, cantered. She pushed off with her back feet, and with Jasmine one her back, she jumped over the bar. While Easy Girl was in midair, Sarah and Jasmine's eyes locked.

Sarah bolted out of the barn.

Lucy, a tall woman with hair twisted in the back to keep it out of her way, had been Sarah's riding teacher for the past year. She followed Sarah into the stable.

Lucy said, "What's up?"

"Nothing."

"I saw you run out of the barn."

With tears running down her cheeks, Sarah said, "I wish I could jump as high as Jasmine."

"Have you forgotten that Jasmine has been riding longer, and works at the barn two days a week? Jasmine thinks like a horse. I don't mean to be too harsh, but I think that sometimes you're in your head too much. But don't worry. We can work on that."

Sarah wiped her tears away

"Tell me," Lucy said, "why is it so important for you to jump?"

"I watched my Aunt Regina ride in horse shows. She gave me her medals to hang in my room. But when I was six, she died of cancer."

"I knew your Aunt Regina. She was a good horsewoman. She would be proud to see how hard you're trying."

Lucy sat down on a wooden bench. "I think part of the reason Jasmine understands horses is because she tracks animals with her dad. When she tracks, she becomes that animal. She's in sixth grade with you, isn't she?"

Sarah nodded. "We're in the same class."

"Jasmine said she was planning to go on some kind of tracking trip with a woman who knows a lot about wild animals. Perhaps you could go with her."

"No way. I don't want to chase a bear or a deer. I like to learn about nature from books. I just want to ride my horse. Anyway, Jasmine is a loner, and she isn't my friend at school."

Sarah rubbed her hands. *Would she ever get any better at riding horses?*

Chapter 2

Cats and Horses

When Sarah arrived home, she searched for Boots, her five-year-old cat. Boots was all black except for his white paws. She peeked under the couch and in the kitchen pantry. After seeing that Boots wasn't there, she climbed the stairs, two steps as a time, to her bedroom. There she found Boots on her bed, luxuriating in the sun.

Sarah picked up the toy she had made for Boots— a feather tied to a string.

She twirled it around, and Boots jumped to get it.

"Oh, Boots. You're so cute, but right now we can't play. I need your help."

She picked him up. "Lucy said if I track animals, I might become a better rider. I don't know if I'll ever be as good as Jasmine."

Sarah looked up and saw the picture on her bureau. It was from the solo she did in her last dance performance. She was on toe, wore a bird costume, and was doing a pirouette. When she danced, she was "in the flow." If only she could feel that way while she was jumping Wind Walker. But riding was different; she had to understand another living being.

Sarah rolled Boots' favorite ball toward the door.

He scampered to get it.

Sarah tried to analyze Boots' steps, but he moved too fast.

She grabbed her brand-new digital camera off her desk, pushed the button to video, and followed Boots down the stairs. She opened the back door, but Boots didn't budge. He rubbed her leg.

"Meow."

Then something moved in the snow covered garden, and he scampered outside.

Sarah grabbed her jacket and slid the door open. Boots jumped up onto the picnic table and then down again, and Sarah filmed Boots as he walked by the lilac bushes. She noticed the round tracks he left in the snow.

After a few minutes, she went back up to her room and downloaded the video to her computer. Sarah, eyes scrunched, watched the clip in slow motion, pausing the video often so she could see Boots' every move. He moved his right rear leg, and then his front left leg—and then his left rear leg followed by his right front leg.

Boots jumped onto her shoulder. Sarah pulled him down and hugged him. "Do you think horses move like you do?" She took a deep sigh. *Jasmine would know.*

When she went down into the kitchen to get something to eat, she passed her older brother Gregg standing at the counter.

Sarah said, "Want to see a video of Boots? I just took it."

"What did you do that for?"

"I thought watching Boots would help me be a better rider."

"I don't get it," Gregg said. He sat down on a kitchen chair with a glass of soda in his hand. "Then again, why should I? You're always weird. You always have your head stuck in a book."

"Stop it."

Gregg said, "Why don't you go to YouTube and watch how horses move?"

"Every once in a while you have a good idea. I mean, every once in a *long* while."

"Whatever."

Sarah went back to the computer, and remembered that before she'd bought Wind Walker, she had watched a video of him online. She still had that page bookmarked, and when the website opened, she pressed the play arrow. She watched Wind Walker's every move, pausing frequently, until she saw the pattern. Walker moved the legs on his right side, and then on his left, not like Boots at all.

She sighed. *Maybe tracking would help, or maybe it wouldn't. Was she willing to take the risk of being teased for spending time with Jasmine?*

Chapter 3

The Choice

The next morning it was bitter cold while Sarah waited for the school bus. She pulled down her fleece hat. Daniel, who went to high school, arrived. Neither of them said hi. He just listened to his iPod.

Sarah turned and saw Jasmine, without a hat, her slightly hunched body pushing against the wind.

When the bus arrived, they all got on. Jasmine sat two rows behind Sarah and stared out the frosted window while Sarah turned to talk to a girl who also studied dance.

When they got off the bus, Sarah greeted her friends from her barn.

Manda said, "I heard Jasmine jumped higher than you can. The stable girl is better than you."

Rachael added, "Why you can't you jump as high as the rest of us?"

"Hey, I thought you were my friends," Sarah replied.

Manda and Rachael walked away giggling.

As the students entered the brightly lit classroom, Ms. Bell, pencil behind her ear, greeted the students. When they'd settled down, Ms. Bell said, "I marked your math homework last night."

She picked up the bundle and handed Jasmine her paper. Ms. Bell gave Jasmine a little pat.

Jasmine stared out the window, as she usually did in school. Sarah knew Jasmine hadn't gotten a good grade.

Ms. Bell handed Sarah her paper, with an A+ in the right-hand corner. "You did an excellent job."

Sarah put the paper into her backpack. *At least she was better than Jasmine in school.*

Ms. Bell said, "I want to go over plans for Winter Break. We're all set for those going skiing. We need one more person to go tracking with Jasmine, and there are too many students signed up to go to Montreal. Anyone willing to volunteer to choose another adventure?"

Bob raised his hand. "I'm willing to go skiing. I had trouble choosing, anyway."

"Anyone else?" Ms. Bell asked. "Jasmine needs someone to go with her. Any takers?"

Sarah was torn. She had wanted to go to Montreal with Manda and Rachael, but now she felt uncomfortable around them.

Ms. Bell said, "We'll just wait and see. Somebody might change his or her mind."

After the kids left the classroom for lunch, when no one was looking, Sarah meandered up to Ms. Bell.

Ms. Bell said, "What's up?"

"Maybe I could go animal tracking?"

"What a surprise. I didn't know you liked the outdoors."

"I don't, but my horseback riding teacher thinks animal tracking would help me ride my horse better. It seems crazy to me, but I'll do anything to become a better rider."

"Just check with your parents, and let me know."

Sarah found Jasmine leaning on a tree at the back of the playground. "I'm thinking about going tracking with you."

"Huh?"

"You need someone to go with you, right?"

"Yeah, but..."

Chapter 4

Into the Woods

Jasmine came home and found her dad all covered with grease, fixing the muffler underneath the log truck. The smell of gasoline filled the air. He called out, "How was your day?"

"It was boring."

"Did you get back your math homework you worked so hard on?"

Jasmine let her muscular body sink down into the garage chair. "I don't want to talk about it."

"All right. We won't."

Jasmine stared out the window, as she often did after school.

Then she sat straight up in the wooden chair. "I may be able to go tracking for Winter Break. Sarah, of all people, said she would go with me. She's one of the smartest kids in our class. She said something about horseback riding and how tracking might help her be a better rider."

"You never know." Her dad patted her shoulder. "Well, I promised you we'd go to the woods today. Why don't you put on some warm clothes and get your snowshoes? I'll get cleaned up."

Jasmine grabbed her metal snowshoes and dashed out to put them into the back of the new pickup truck.

When they arrived at the woods, Jasmine put on her snowshoes. As she sprinted into the forest, she heard the chatter of red squirrels among the pine, spruce, and fir. The branches of the trees sheltered her from the wind.

The snow sounded like crunching potato chips under her feet, and the branches danced a slow waltz.

Jasmine said, "Do you see those prints near that white pine tree? Can we follow them?"

"Sure," her father replied.

There were two footprints next to each other, and then a space before the next pair of tracks. Larger and larger spaces came between the pairs of track—until the tracks were about the length of a yard stick.

Jasmine said, "I can't believe how far apart these tracks are. This animal was moving fast."

Another set of tracks crossed their path.

Jasmine's dad said, "We'll come back and follow them later."

The two of them quickened their pace, and finally there was a small patch of ice covered with a thin layer of snow.

Jasmine said, "The tracks are webbed. It looks like a duck, but ducks don't jump, and I can see a few hairs in this print."

The land began to dip steeply toward a pond, and there were no longer prints. Instead, there was a smooth depression, the width of a toboggan that went down the hill.

Jasmine sat down in the path and slid down the hill with her legs lifted high.

"Wee!" she roared. "This animal was having fun."

When they got to the pond, they saw the animal they'd been following.

"It's an otter," Jasmine said.

"Yup!"

The otter dove down into a hole in the ice and disappeared.

They laughed as they followed their tracks back up the hill, until they reached the set of prints they'd seen earlier.

Jasmine's dad bent down. "The tracks are in a straight line. This animal was on a mission. No fooling around here like a dog."

"If you look closely," he continued, "you can see that each print shows the animal had four toes and claws. The prints are on the small side, so their probably from a fox."

Jasmine looked up at her father and smiled. *He knew so much. She wished she could be so smart.*

He said, "Let's see what he was up to. He's trotting as only a fox can. He moved his two front feet and then his back feet. His head was straight ahead, but his body was perpendicular to the way he was traveling."

Jasmine said, "The fox must move smoother than a horse when it trots. A horse moves opposite feet at the same time—left back and right front—and it feels bumpy unless you post."

"You know a lot about horses."

Then they saw that each series of four tracks made an elongated C with the back feet making the upper part of the curve and the front feet the lower part.

Jasmine's dad said, "The fox started to gallop."

"Do you think he was spooked?"

She imaged the animal with all four feet in the air, like a horse moving at top speed.

Up ahead, there stood a six-foot-tall wire fence with square holes, each side the length of a magic marker. The tracks went to the fence and then continued on the other side.

Jasmine said, "Foxes don't climb fences, but he didn't fit through that hole. It's too small. I don't get it."

"A fox is skinnier than you think. He went through it. All that fur makes him look fatter than he is."

Jasmine stared at the other side of the fence. "I wish we could climb over to the other side. What do you think happened next?"

"We'll never know, but there are always new mysteries to solve."

Back at the house, in the bedroom Jasmine shared with her two sisters, she took her favorite sketch pad out of her backpack. She drew the otter while she lay on her bed next to the window.

Her dad opened the door to her bedroom. "What are you drawing?"

She showed him the sketches.

"That's exactly what the otter looked like. You're quite the artist."

Jasmine closed her sketchbook. *Maybe I can draw, but I'm a loser in school*, she thought.

Chapter 5

Meeting Tess

Sarah came home from school and found her mom on the living room sofa.

Sarah took off her down jacket. "Can I go tracking for Winter Break? Jasmine is going."

"I thought you wanted to go to Montreal, and since when do you hang out with Jasmine?"

"I wanted to go to Montreal, but Lucy said maybe I could jump like Aunt Regina if I learned how to track animals."

"I don't get it, there could be bears in the woods, but I trust Lucy. Let's talk to dad tonight."

That night Sarah hid behind her parents' door. She listened as they talked about her possibly going on the trip with the tracking lady, and she peaked through the crack between the door and the door frame. Her mom sat stiffly in bed, her hair up in curlers, as she leaned against the headboard. "Sarah wants to go tracking for Winter Break."

"That sounds great," Sarah's father responded. "I have always wanted her to spend more time outdoors. She's always dancing, horseback riding, or reading. I think it would be good for her."

"Sarah said something about staying with a woman named Tess who is supposed to be a great tracker. Do you know her?"

Sarah's dad stroked his wife's leg. "I used to go fishing with Tess and her husband. He died two years ago. I don't think they ever had children. Maybe that's the reason she wants to share her love for the woods. She learned what she knows from her grandmother, who was a Native American."

"If she hasn't raised children, how does she know how to deal with them—especially preteens? I don't know." She fixed a curler that had fallen out. "I want to meet her before I let Sarah stay there for two nights. If it doesn't look safe, I'm going to have to insist that she comes home. I called Jasmine's dad today, and he said he would be happy to drive, but I'll tell him I would be glad to bring the girls."

"I'm sure it will be okay," Sarah's father said, "but you go ahead and check it out for yourself. I trust your judgment."

Tess lived in the northern, isolated section of town, where the forest grew tall with spruce, maple, and hemlock.

When they arrived, Sarah's mom used the shiny brass knocker on the front door of the log house. A sturdy-looking woman with flowing gray hair opened the door. She was wearing green woolen pants with a red plaid flannel shirt, and she seemed ready to go into the woods.

"Come in," she said. "I'm Tess." The girls put their snowshoes on the front porch next to a neatly stacked pile of wood while Sarah's mom stepped forward.

"This is my daughter, Sarah, and her friend Jasmine, and I'm Helen." She smiled as she looked at Tess's soft face. "What a nice place you have here. I wish my house could be so neat." Sarah's mom smiled again when she walked into the living room and saw Tess's library.

Sarah noticed a number of pelts hanging from the wall, a bear's foot that was the base of a lamp, and a deer head mounted over the fireplace. She turned her head away, a little disgusted. *She must have been crazy to choose tracking for her Winter Break trip. She would have been much happier going to Montreal. It was weird, but her mom didn't seem worried now. She couldn't let her mom know it, but she was a little nauseated.*

Helen said, "Goodbye, girls. I can't wait to hear about your adventures. Be safe, and call if you need me. I'll pick you up on Wednesday afternoon."

Tess stood in the alcove and closed the door after Sarah's mother left. "It's so great to have you here," she said to the girls. "I hear you're both horse lovers. I used to ride when I was your age. Helped me be a better tracker." She went to the window, and then said, "The sleet has ended, so we'll be able to go into the woods today. But first let me show you to your room."

The girls put their bags on their shoulders and climbed up the wooden stairs. Sarah noticed that each of the bunk beds had a beautiful blanket glowing with the light that poured in from the window. Not knowing what else to talk about, she said, "Look at all those animals on the blankets."

Tess replied, "My grandmother wove these coverings. She was from the Abenaki tribe. Why don't you get settled and come on down when you're ready."

After Tess had left, Sarah whispered, "Did you see that bear's foot? It gave me the creeps. What do you think of Tess?"

"She seems okay. Where did she get all those things from—maybe her grandma?"

"That's cool if her grandmother took her into the woods, but I'm not sure what I think about her."

A few moments later Tess called up the stairs, "Girls, are you ready to go outside?"

Chapter 6

Snowshoeing in Tess's Woods

Wisps of clouds decorated the sky, looking like all sorts of things—flying saucers, flying geese, and chariots.

Sarah watched Jasmine put her snowshoes on and tried to copy her, but the strap kept coming loose. She twisted and turned the bindings until her foot fit snugly. *Maybe this is too much for me*, she thought. *Maybe we'll get lost.*

Tess put on her wooden snowshoes, the old-fashioned kind with leather strapping.

Sarah stood up. "I've never used these snowshoes."

"I know, but it's really easy," Jasmine said. "All you do is walk."

Sarah took her first few steps. *This isn't too bad*, she thought, but then she felt her snowshoe catch, and she lost her balance, falling backward into the snow. Her wool hat landed in a nearby snowdrift. She bit her lip. "I thought you said it was really easy," she said to Jasmine.

Jasmine reached down to pull Sarah up, and fell over herself. "You crossed the backs of your snowshoes," Jasmine said. "Keep your feet wide apart."

Sarah preferred the toe shoes she wore in ballet class. She took a deep breath, rolled onto her side, pulled her knees in, and pushed herself against the snow. When she was standing again, she brushed herself off and picked up her hat.

They were standing at the beginning of a narrow wooded trail that Tess had packed down the day before. "I use this trail so often," Tess told them, her voice crisp and clear, "that I could almost walk it blindfolded."

"Why don't you go last," Tess said to Sarah. "The snow will be packed down even more, and it will make it easier for you to walk. You go first, Jasmine. You'll enjoy that."

The path was even, but the forest surrounding them seemed dark to Sarah. The snow hung on the lower branches of the trees. In places, the branches drooped down so low that the three trackers had to bend down.

Near a huge spruce, Jasmine pointed to a large animal print in the wet snow. They clustered around it.

Sarah placed her snowshoe next to the track. "Whoa. It's about the size of my foot. It couldn't be a bear, could it?" She took several steps back. Her mother was right. There were bears in the woods. But she would never let her mother know she was scared.

"Follow the track," Tess said, "and see where it goes."

Sarah and Jasmine both looked all around, but they couldn't find another print.

"What do you think the story is about this track?" Tess asked.

Sarah looked down at the track and then at Tess. "What do you mean by 'the story'?"

Tess brushed off her wool coat. "I mean, what do you think happened?"

Sarah looked up at the rough tree bark. "Maybe the bear climbed down the tree and took one step before it went up again?"

Jasmine said, "Maybe so."

Tess chuckled and pointed up to a nearby tree that still had its needles. The branches sagged with snow.

"Oh." Sarah looked up and put her hands on her hips. "The snow fell down from that tree. What a relief."

Tess smiled. "That's what I call a tree track. I learned that from my grandmother."

Sarah tightened the straps on her snowshoe. "Is that how you learned about the woods?"

"I used to stay with her when my parents went away. She took me out into the woods and taught me how to track in the winter and find medicinal plants in the spring and summer, and she taught me how to ride horses."

"What did your grandmother look like?" asked Jasmine.

"She was big, with shiny black hair she wore in a band made out of feathers." Tess grinned. "She made the nicest baskets in the village, with wonderful patterns. They called her Anaskemezi, 'Oak Tree,' because she was so strong in her heart."

They continued on the trail, the path starting to lead slightly uphill, and Sarah wondered where she should look. She watched Jasmine glancing in all directions as she walked, taking in information from everywhere. Jasmine looked so comfortable in the woods.

Then Jasmine stopped. A set of tracks crossed their path.

Sarah pointed. "That's weird. There's a group of four prints, then a space, and then four more prints. In each group, the larger prints are ahead of the smaller ones."

"It pushed off with its big back feet, landed on its two front feet and swung the back feet around to push off again," Tess said.

Sarah tried to follow the tracks with her eyes. "That's got to be a rabbit hopping, right?"

"Follow the tracks," Tess told her.

Sarah walked a short distance to where the tracks ended at a tree. They appeared again on the other side of the tree.

"I guess it's not a rabbit," Sarah said. "I've never seen a picture, in any of my books, of a rabbit climbing a tree. What could it be?"

They followed the tracks for twenty more feet and came to a hole about the size of a plum. Little piles of soil and leaves lay on top of the snow.

Jasmine leaned down and put her head close to the hole. "It's a squirrel. They hide their food in the fall. He must be digging it up."

Tess nodded. "It's a gray squirrel."

"They have big back feet, right?" Sarah said. "Their legs sure must be strong. It would be fun to be able to jump up in the air like that. Almost like jumping a horse."

They went on up the trail. Jasmine, out in front, stopped at another set of prints. The three trackers gathered around the impressions.

Sarah said, "They're deep and arranged in a straight line."

Like a detective gathering clues, Jasmine bent down, took off her glove, and used her hand to feel the slightly melted print.

"What are you doing?" Sarah asked.

"I'm trying to feel the shape of the track. My dad taught me you can feel better than you can see when it's icy, but it's too soft today."

At least she doesn't know what kind of animal it is, Sarah thought. *She knows everything else. But what kind of animal is it? Should she be worried?*

"Can we follow these tracks?" Jasmine asked. "Even though we'll have to leave the trail?"

A gush of wind almost blew Jasmine's hat off, but she pushed it back down.

Tess waved her hand for them to continue following the impressions the animal had made in the snow.

"Are we following it?" Sarah asked. "Or going to where it came from?"

Tess said, "We'll try to follow it. Who knows? We might have a chance to see it. You can tell which way it traveled because the front of the track is usually deeper than the back."

They moved in a line, with Jasmine still in the lead.

For the first time ever, Sarah was walking through the forest without being on a trail. Now they entered a spruce forest. The trees grew very close together. At eye height, one could see only snow-covered branches.

"These branches have prickly needles," Sarah said. "I didn't expect the woods to be as thick as a jungle." Her breath was fast, and shallow. *We might get lost*, she thought. *Maybe she shouldn't have chosen tracking for Winter Break. Maybe this was just too much of a challenge.*

"When you move through these woods, thick with small trees, leave a bit of space behind me, and move slow-ly," Tess said. "That will stop the branches from snapping back at you."

Sarah nodded. "Can we get lost?"

"Don't worry about getting lost, because we can always turn around and follow our tracks back."

Sarah said, "Oh, yeah. I hadn't thought of that."

She followed Tess's instructions, and when she slowed

down, her breathing slowed down, too. The branches no longer hurt. Sarah thought that Tess was actually kind of nice.

Tess pointed at the girls' feet and said, "You've been very good at not walking on any prints. If you did, you'd accidently destroy the clues a detective uses to solve a mystery."

Jasmine whispered as if to herself, "This is a mystery."

Chapter 7

Following Tracks

They walked slowly because the heavy, soggy snow made it hard to lift up their snowshoes.

Sarah was starting to feel tired. She leaned against the nearest hemlock tree, until she realized her jacket was getting dirty.

After moving forward a few more steps, they finally came to a print they could read. The track had a hoof mark in it.

Jasmine said, "It's a deer?"

Tess said, "Yes. That's the only animal that has a hoof around here, except for a moose. But it's too small for a moose."

The followed the tracks up the easiest terrain, a well-worn path made by many deer over the decades.

Then they came to a roundish depression about a yard long.

Jasmine said, "I think it's a deer bed. My dad said deer lie down to rest. They curl up. This one is small. It must be a fawn."

"How can it lie down on this cold snow?" Sarah asked. "The poor fawn must have been freezing."

Tess replied, "When we get back to the house, you can feel the thick deer skin and the dense fur of one of my pelts. That will help you understand how the fawn stayed warm."

Jasmine bent down, found a few short brown hairs, and showed them to Sarah.

Sarah could feel how thick the hair felt. "This is much

thicker than Boots' hair. I could see how it could help keep the deer warm."

"I've read that fawns are born in late spring," Sarah said. "This fawn would be"—she counted on her fingers—"about eight months old."

They continued to follow the tracks the fawn had made after it had woken up. The tracks were no longer evenly spaced nor in a straight line. They looked like the tracks of someone who was drunk. Farther along, the girls found four hoof prints close together, next to a deep depression the size of the fawn's body. Then the tracks continued.

Sarah tightened her shoulders. "I think the fawn stumbled and fell." She knew what it felt like to lose her balance. She often did when she was trying to jump Walker, but she had never fallen off.

Tess said, "What do you want to do? Should we keep following it? We could find something upsetting."

Sarah hesitated. She didn't want to see anything gory, but she asked, "Do you think we could help?"

"Maybe," Tess said. "We won't know unless we follow the tracks."

Jasmine continued up the hill. Sarah and Tess followed a few steps behind. The spaces between trees became wider, and the trees became older, which made it easier for the trackers to snowshoe. However, the fawn's path had prints close together.

"This fawn is sick. Why?" Jasmine said.

Tess thought for a moment, and then said, "They can get viruses or bacterial infections, like pneumonia, just like us."

A little ways up ahead, large deep prints, in a straight

line, joined the fawn trail. When Sarah peered into these prints, she saw that they were heart-shaped. Sarah said, "The mother deer must have heard its fawn crying for help. Maybe things will turn out all right."

Jasmine looked through the needled branches and pointed excitedly to a point in the distance. She whispered, "I can see a fawn by that large spruce tree."

They moved forward, but the fawn didn't run away.

They moved closer. From ten feet away they saw the reddish brown fawn ripped apart, with its organs exposed and blood everywhere. Leaves that had been dug up partially covered it. A strong putrid smell filled the air.

Sarah gasped. She wanted to vomit. She whispered, "This is disgusting. I'm feeling sick." She slumped down on top of the snow.

"This is horrible to look at," Tess said. "Are you okay, Sarah?" Sarah didn't answer.

"How are you, Jasmine?"

"I don't know."

"At least this deer was sick and then an animal put it out of its misery and not because a dog chased it. Dogs have extra energy because they are fed, so they can outrun deer and maim them for life. Then dogs are likely to hound other deer."

Ravens circled, waiting for the trackers to leave.

The deer mother's tracks circled the fawn.

Sarah stared at the prints until they were so far away that she couldn't see them.

Sarah said, "The mother must be so upset. I would be. I'd like to go back to your house."

Then suddenly Jasmine said, "By the fawn's head. There's something I can't make out in the snow."

Chapter 8

Tracking the Predator

Sarah could see more blood. *Oh, no*, she thought, *something else to worry about.*

"These tracks don't look like deer tracks," Tess said.

Jasmine and Tess moved around the fawn to see the tracks, while Sarah stayed still. The two of them stepped softly and silently as if they were in a church.

"These are old tracks. Why don't we follow them?" Tess said.

Sarah turned white. "I think I want to go back. I'm grossed out. Anyway, why do you want to follow the tracks?"

"Following the tracks can help us understand the life of the forest," Tess said, "but we don't have to go if you don't want to."

Sarah surprised herself. A desire to know what animal had killed the deer came over her. But she said, "I'm scared about following this animal."

"No need to worry. I know the prints are old," Tess said. "It looks like they're about a day old. Look, you can see that my tracks are much clearer, with more detail. Look at this print. All the edges are melted. They're not like the crisp marks on my track. Do you remember the sleet we had this morning? If you look into these tracks, you will see pockmarks. Those are from the sleet. So this animal was here before this morning."

The three trackers followed the prints up through the exposed ledges. The snow made the ledges slippery, so they grabbed trees and used them to pull themselves up. They came upon a crevice in the rocks that made the ledges easier to climb, but they still needed to use trees to support themselves.

Jasmine said to Sarah, "Take my hand."

"No. I'm all right. When I was in circus camp, I used to shimmy up tall poles."

Soon they found a clear track. A hemlock tree with low hanging branches held up some of the snow. Sarah and Jasmine bent down to take a closer look at the animal's track. The print had four toes and no claw marks, and one toe looked longer than the rest.

Sarah said, "It's twice the size of Boots' prints."

They both turned to Tess. Tess said, "You are right. It's some kind of cat."

Sarah took a little gulp of air and said, "Is it a mountain lion?"

Tess shook her head. "That would be about three times the size."

Sarah squatted to look at the tracks a little more closely. "Then, it might be a bobcat. I've read about them in a nature series book." She added, "They hunt small mammals, and I guess this bobcat easily killed the sick fawn. That's so wrong."

The wind had picked up. Tess took a few more steps and stopped at a circle about two feet wide with two long depressions on either side of it. She bent down. "This track is rare. What do you think the bobcat was doing?"

Jasmine said, "It's where the bobcat sat when he saw the fawn—like how a cat sits when it waits for a mouse or a bird."

Sarah said, "It's like I was sitting at the edge of a chair ready to jump out of my seat."

Sarah looked down at her snowshoes. "I'm so angry at my cat if he kills a bird. I can't believe I'm saying this, but if I was a hungry bobcat, I would've eaten that sick deer, too."

Jasmine added, "If the fawn had died from the infection, it would have probably died slowly. The bobcat helped the fawn not hurt for so long."

Tess said, "This is hard stuff. It might take a while to understand what happened. I've been in the woods since I was a little kid, but I only started understanding how nature works when I was sixteen."

The three of them stood in silence for a few moments. Then Tess said, "Are you ready to go?"

They went back down the hill, to an overhang where the ground was level, and Tess said, "Why don't we take a break."

Jasmine and Sarah were dressed in snow pants, so they could sit in the snow. Tess pulled out a plastic garbage bag she had brought so she wouldn't get her wool pants wet. They sunk into the snow and placed their legs over the rocky outcrop.

Tess said, "Here's some lunch I packed for you."

Sarah didn't feel like eating, but she nervously gobbled up the homemade brownies, and the brown crumbs fell onto the snow.

They ate in silence.

From where they sat, they could look out and see part of their town. A few houses dotted the woods and open fields. Everything looked so small.

"Can we see our houses?" Sarah asked.

"Not from here," Jasmine said. "They're behind that ridge."

Sarah wished she had known that, but she thought, *at least she had figured out the age of the fawn.*

They decided to return to Tess's house, and when they could, they slid downhill.

Back at the house, the girls, who were all tuckered out, went into the living room. Tess found the deer skin. "Why don't you feel this hide," she said, and passed it to Sarah.

"It sure is thick and dense, just like you said. I just remembered last year I Googled to find out about Native Americans for a report I was writing for school. I learned they made clothes out of deerskin to stay warm. Did your grandmother wear deerskin?"

"She wore a wraparound skirt made from it."

Jasmine studied the skin, turning it back and forth.

In their bedroom, Sarah read her book. Jasmine drew the dead fawn and how she pictured the bobcat looked.

When Sarah finished, she got up to brush her hair. She looked at Jasmine's drawing.

"I wish I could draw like you."

"I wish I could do math as good as you."

Sarah said, "It comes easy to me." She finished brushing her hair. She thought, *Being in the woods doesn't come easy to me.* She hoped they could rest tonight.

Chapter 9

Owling

After they finished eating, Tess said, "Why don't we go for a walk to the wetland where owls sometimes hunt. It's a full moon out tonight, so we'll be able to see."

"I'd like to go," Jasmine said.

"I brought my flashlight along, but I didn't expect to use it," Sarah said, shrugging her shoulders. She didn't want to ask if they might run into a bat. That would be scary.

"If you don't want to go out," Tess said, "we can stay here and play cards or something."

Sarah trusted Tess more since she had been helpful earlier that day. Tess seemed to understand her. Sarah said, "I'll go with you. I wish I could ride Wind Walker. He's so good seeing at night. Anyway, I've never seen an owl."

They dressed warmly because of the cold night air.

Tess said, "The best way to see an owl is to walk silently. I will try to call in a barred owl."

Sarah placed herself in the middle, so she would feel safer. They walked in the opposite direction from the path they had taken in the morning. This flatter trail made walking easier. The full moon shone through the delicate clouds, but even still, it took a few minutes for their eyes to adjust to the darkness.

Sarah began to see cattails moving to and fro. She had learned from one of her nature books that cattails grow in marshes and swamps, so she knew they had arrived at a wetland. The sky opened up, and the stars lit up the winter sky. When she looked down, she saw tiny tunnels in the snow. She wondered what had made them.

The night sounded still, until Tess cupped her mouth and called out, her a voice resonating with rich sounds. It sounded like, "Who cooks for you? Who cooks for you aaaall?"

They waited patiently. Tess called again, but again there was no answer. Each time she called, she faced a different direction. Sarah's feet felt cold, but she stood still.

The fifth time she called, there came a soft reply, from the distance. "Who cooks for you? Who cooks for you aaaall?" The girls gave each other a silent high five. Sarah's eyes became big. She strained her ears to listen. She had never heard such a beautiful, yet ghostly sound. Tess didn't stop, but answered the owl's call. The owl's response got louder and louder, and Sarah and Jasmine continued to stand quietly. Tess sounded just like the owl. Sarah had read in a book, *Owl Moon that* an owl's flight was silent, so she knew they wouldn't be able to hear it fly. As she finished her thought, she gasped as she saw the large wings of the owl. It flew onto a branch of a red oak tree that towered over the wetland. By the light of the moon, Sarah could make out that the owl was bigger than she had thought. It had striking black and white horizontal stripes, and its eyes looked black. Sarah didn't dare take another breath. She could tell by the smile on Jasmine's face that she saw it, too.

It stopped answering Tess when it landed in the tree next to them, as if to say, "I don't cook for you. You're not another owl."

The night fell silent again.

After they all arrived home, and were finally able to talk, the girls jabbered about the owl. Sarah said, "That was so cool. Have you been able to call an owl in before?"

"Yes" Tess answered, "many times. It isn't hard. It just takes practice. I learned how to call from my grandma. She taught me during the winter, which is when they mate, and so they were more talkative."

Jasmine took off her mittens, and as she put her hands to her chin, she said, "Can you teach me to call an owl?"

Tess clapped her hands to the beat of the barred owl's call, and then Jasmine hooted. Sarah danced out the rhythm.

Tess said, "You're quick learners.

When they arrived home, Sarah took off her mittens, and walked upstairs to her bedroom, glad they hadn't seen a bat.

Chapter 10

To the Pond

The next morning Sarah and Jasmine woke up as the sun lit up their east-facing window. At breakfast, Sarah asked, "What are the plans for today. No more dead animals!"

Tess said, "Don't worry. We'll try to go and look for some living animals at a frozen pond. It's a little uphill, but pretty when you get there. Perhaps we'll see a moose."

Sarah put on her snowshoes. She didn't need her hat, so she put in her pocket. She wondered whether moose ever charged at people.

They walked on the same trail as they had during the day before, but continued past the point where they had first encountered the fawn's tracks.

Tess pulled down a branch and took out her knife.

Jasmine said, "That knife looks really old."

"I found it in a stone-walled cellar hole."

Sarah said, "What's a cellar hole?"

"A cellar hole is from a house built by white people. The wooden part rotted away and left behind the stone. But that's not how my people lived. My grandmother used to tell me, her grandmother lived in a wigwam made out of saplings covered with birch bark."

Tess cut three pieces from the branch.

Tess surprised Sarah when she said, "As far as I know, all trees are edible in this area, though some taste better than others."

"People eat trees?" Sarah said, laughing.

"That would be strange," said Tess. "What I meant is

they eat the twigs, the fruit, and sometimes the sap. Try chewing this black birch twig."

Jasmine took the small branch in her mouth and chewed slowly. Sarah shook her head. She did not want to eat trees.

"You don't have to eat it. How about just smelling it?" Tess asked.

Sarah brought the branch close to her nose. "Minty."

Jasmine added, "It tastes good."

When no one was looking, Sarah threw the twig to the ground. It might have smelled and even tasted like mint, but she still didn't want to eat it.

Tess said, "Let's keep walking so we can stay warm."

They came upon some fresh tracks. Sarah said excitedly as she raised her voice and pointed, "Hey, a new print. I don't think we've seen this one before."

Four prints marked the snow. Then there was a space, and four more prints. Within each set the larger prints made by the back feet were ahead of the smaller front feet.

Sarah said, "This looks like the squirrel tracks from yesterday, but much bigger. It must have moved just like the squirrel did, too, but because the prints are so much bigger, it must be a rabbit. I had no idea rabbits could have such big back feet."

"It's a snowshoe hare," Tess said.

Sarah laughed heartily. "I get it. They have big feet like I do with my snowshoes on, except it would be hard for me to hop."

Tess laughed, too. "And they can hop really far. Let's see if we can follow their tracks." With difficulty, they used their snowshoes to push aside dense thickets of spruce saplings.

They watched the tracks closely until they started

to see little round brown balls, about half the size of a grape.

Jasmine said, "I'm pretty sure it must be rabbit poop. It looks like the poop from my cousin's rabbit."

Tess said, "The snowshoe hare might be hiding anywhere around here, and we'd never know it, because it sits so still. The tracks and scat look fresh, but we've probably made enough noise to scare it away."

Sarah added, "I've read that hares turn white in the winter so they're camouflaged against the snow."

Sarah started to look, but then stopped. "Won't they bite us?"

"No need to worry," said Tess. "They eat twigs in the winter, just like we did."

Sarah continued her searching in all directions under the needled branches. She was disappointed because she had no luck, and she thought, *It would be easier to find Boots. At least he has a black body.*

The threesome continued uphill. "Phew," Sarah said, and she unzipped her jacket.

They heard a hollow sound, like a drummer hitting two sticks together as fast as he could. As they walked up the trail that followed the stream, the noise became louder, the rhythm more predictable. Sarah had never heard that kind of sound before—so loud. Jasmine circled in place and tried to locate the sound. She scanned the tops of the trees.

She said, "A very large bird is flying from tree to tree." And just then, the sun caught the bird's bright red head. "Wow." Jasmine said as she motioned with her green mittens to show Tess and Sarah where to look.

"That's a pileated woodpecker," said Tess.

As she tilted her head back, Sarah said, "Where?"

"In the tree with a fork," replied Jasmine. "To the right of the pine tree."

Sarah got only a glimpse of the bird as it flew away. Disappointed, she tapped her snowshoe, envious of how much Jasmine could observe.

Tess said, "From here to the pond, we will need to cross the brook at a small wooden bridge and then walk steeply uphill."

When they got to the bridge, Tess scratched her head. "This brook is usually frozen solid this time of year."

Sarah heard ice cracking.

They easily walked over the simply built bridge.

The threesome continued on the rocky steep trail, which followed the brook. As they got closer to the pond, the ice disappeared and the resonating sound of the brook got louder, too.

"Something is wrong," Tess said. "We need to leave. A section of the beaver dam must have broken. The flowing water makes it impossible to cross here. I hope we can get back to the bridge before it's too late."

Sarah moved away from the brook. If only she had stayed home, she could have been reading a book now and snuggling with Boots.

Tess sprinted, taking very long steps along the over-flowing banks of the brook. The girls followed. They descended as fast as they could, but the water flowed faster and the water roared.

When they got near the bridge, Tess shook her head and yelled, "It's moving so fast we can't go back the way we came."

Sarah couldn't believe it. There was no longer a bridge, only remnants of logs strewn on the snow.

Chapter 11

Crossing the Brook

The trio walked along the brook. Tess said, "Let's make sure our snowshoes don't get wet. Otherwise, they'll freeze and become heavy."

The water rose and the bank disappeared.

As usual, Sarah followed Tess and Jasmine. About a hundred feet ahead, Sarah noticed that a large pine tree lay across the brook. Sarah lifted one snowshoe to get onto the log, found her balance, and raised the other leg. Sarah awkwardly took to two steps and walked over a branch stub.

She yelled out over the booming sound of the water, "You can cross the brook on this log."

Tess twisted her body and yelled, "Come back. It isn't safe!"

Sarah said, "No, I'm safe." She knew she could cross on this flat log, because in dance class, everyone called her the balance queen. Sarah took a few more steps, and then she started to wobble.

Tess rushed to the log and said, "You must return."

"I can't turn around," Sarah said. "I'll have to go to the other side and then come back."

Tess shouted above the deafening sound of the brook, "Take off your snowshoes before you come back. The snow is shallow enough."

Tess didn't take her eyes off Sarah until she returned. "We need to figure out a plan."

They huddled together near a group of sugar maples.

Jasmine said, "I'm afraid to walk on that tree."

Tess said, "It's hard for me, too. I think both of us need to take off our snowshoes and ford the brook. We'll give them to Sarah, and we'll cross holding onto the log." She bent down and easily took off her snowshoes. She continued, "There's no other place to cross. Downstream it turns into a waterfall. This is the best we can do. We'll get wet, but we'll make a fire when we get home."

Sarah straightened up. "I have a better plan. One at a time, you can hold on to my shoulders, and I can help you cross this brook. You won't get wet that way."

Tess shook her head. "No. I don't think that's safe. We should stick to my plan."

Sarah said, "But I know I can do it."

Tess went to the edge of the brook and put her leather boot in. She called back, "It's deeper than I thought."

She stepped back onto the bank.

Turning to Sarah, Tess said, "These woods have been scary for you, but you seem so confident. Are you sure you're up to this?"

Sarah said, "You have to believe me. I know I can help both of you cross the log. I was the best tightwire walker in circus camp." Sarah spread her arms out to show them how she would balance. "I learned to walk on a wire by putting my hands on my teacher's shoulders. I know this will work."

"Jasmine," Tess said, "are you okay with this?"

She nodded and took off her snowshoes.

"I'm going to trust you," Tess told Sarah. "You can place Jasmine's snowshoes between your back and your backpack."

"Good," Sarah said. "Then I can keep my arms free to help me balance."

As Jasmine handed the snowshoes to Tess, they fell out of her arms.

"I'll pick the snowshoes up," said Tess. "Turn around, Sarah."

Tess shoved them into place.

Sarah tightened the straps of her backpack and walked back and forth. "It's good."

"Be safe," said Tess.

Sarah straightened out her jacket and walked onto the log. "Are you game?" Sarah asked Jasmine, who nodded and gently placed her hands onto Sarah's shoulders.

What if this doesn't work? Sarah wondered. Even though she had practiced in camp, she was a little scared. It was one thing to walk on a wire over a mat, but another to have rocks below you and have someone touching your shoulders.

"Are you ready? Don't look down but at the back of my head," Sarah told Jasmine.

Jasmine squeezed Sarah's shoulders. She forced herself to look at Sarah's brown hair.

Slowly they began to make their way across the brook. When Sarah moved her right foot, so did Jasmine. When Sarah moved her left foot, Jasmine moved hers. To get over the branch stub, Sarah leaned toward the right. She said, "Are you all right?"

"I'm a little scared," said Jasmine, and she held on to Sarah's shoulders more firmly.

"We've made it more than halfway. We can do it."

"Watch out. Your water bottle is falling out of the backpack's side pocket."

They heard a loud crash when the plastic container hit a rock.

Sarah took a deep breath. *At least it wasn't either of them.*

She said, "Keep focusing on me." Sarah couldn't see Jasmine, but she felt her eyes burning into the back of her head.

When they reached the other side, they jumped up and clasped each other's mittens.

Sarah said, "I'll be right back."

For the fourth time, Sarah walked over the log. She hoped her luck would hold up. It was so much easier walking alone.

The brook roared louder, and branches flowed under the tree bridge.

When she returned to the other side, she bent down to pick up Tess's snowshoes.

"No need to do that. I'm all right with them on my back.

Tess, slightly taller than Sarah, scooped up her wooden snowshoes.

Sarah shoved the snowshoes in the right place and Tess tightened her straps. She centered her green cloth backpack and softly touched Sarah's shoulders for balance.

"We have to be extra careful," Sarah said. "I've pushed off all the snow and it's slippery. Are you ready? Look at the back of my head, just like Jasmine did."

"I'm ready."

Sarah stepped onto the downed tree, and Tess was right behind. They followed the same rhythm; their two feet were together on the right and then on the left, moving in unison.

They were three quarters of the way there when Sarah heard a loud sound. She tried to ignore it, but it was making such a racquet that she looked up. A hawk flew by, with a crow chasing it.

"Are you feeling steady?" Tess asked.

"Don't worry. We're fine." She was glad this was the last time she had to cross on this fallen tree. At least she hoped it was the last time.

Sarah stepped off the log.

When Tess stepped onto solid ground, she bowed ever so slightly. "Thank you so very much."

They put on their snowshoes and started back toward the house, Tess said, "Your parents will be astonished when they hear of our adventure. As my grandma always said, "The woods are not to be feared but respected."

A black-capped chickadee flew onto a nearby branch, and the three of them smiled. When they arrived home, Tess brought in some wood to make a fire. Sarah, Jasmine and Tess leaned back on their chairs as they watched the flames dance.

That night Sarah had a dream about Boots. It was a surprising one, but she soon forgot it.

Chapter 12

More Tracking Adventures

Early the next morning, they sat at a wooden table, eating the omelet Tess had prepared. Jasmine said, "Is the place where you found the old knife, that cellar hole, far away?"

"No. It's within walking distance."

Jasmine said, "Can we go there?"

Tess looked surprised, but said, "Sure, if Sarah is up to it."

Sarah said, "I'm tired." She ate another bite of eggs. "I would love to read the next chapter in *My Side of the Mountain,* but I'll try to get myself psyched to go. Is a cellar hole something you can fall into?"

"Even in the snow, you can see the edge of the stones, so it isn't dangerous," Tess said. "Why don't you get ready for the woods? Since today's our last day together, it would be good to get an early start."

"It can't be the last day already," said Sarah.

Jasmine looked down at the ground. "This is so much more fun than school."

Sarah said, "I can help you with math when we get back."

As they put on their warm clothes, Sarah said, "What were you drawing last night?"

"You and Tess on that dead tree bridge."

"Can I look at it?"

Jasmine pulled out the sketch pad. Sarah and Tess both huddled around the drawing.

"I can't believe you drew this," Sarah said as she took the drawing pad from Jasmine's hand.

"It's only a sketch. You can have it, Tess."

"Are you sure?"

Jasmine tore out the page and handed it to Tess.

By now, it was easy for Sarah to get her snowshoes on. She remembered back to the first time. That seemed years ago.

They took the same trail but turned uphill at the sugar maple tree instead of continuing on to the brook. From there on, they walked in a deciduous forest with only dried leaves left on the beech trees.

Tracks from hopping creatures covered the forest floor. Sarah followed the impressions with her eyes, and noticed that sometimes, near a tree, the tracks went under the snow.

Sarah said, "They're much, much smaller than a squirrel track. I think it's a mouse." Pointing at the small skinny impression that marked the middle of the tracks, she said, "Looks like it's dragging its feet."

"It can't be feet," Jasmine said. "It's the tail."

"It has a very long tail, too," said Tess.

Sarah thought, *Jasmine is right again, but that's okay. At least I helped her yesterday.*

They followed the trail uphill and saw a stone wall that paralleled the trail. Sarah noticed tracks of an animal that had climbed over the wall to their side.

Jasmine said, "These footprints are different. There are only two next to each other, and then two more far away. That's cool."

"It's moving like an accordion because it has such a long body. For a moment, the four feet are in the air. Any guesses?" asked Tess.

Sarah said, "I don't have a clue."

Jasmine bent down. "It looks like the otter tracks I followed with my dad, but these prints aren't webbed."

"If we can find a clear print, you'll figure it out," Tess said.

Finally, on one of the rocks of the stone wall, a print outline showed clearly in the snow.

Tess said, "Count the toes."

"It looks like five of them," said Sarah. "It can't be a cat or dog."

"Well, I know what it isn't," Jasmine said, "but I don't know what it is."

Tess answered, "That's always a good start. I'll tell you. It's a fisher. It's a kind of weasel."

Both girls shook their heads, and Tess continued, "It's like a mink, only bigger. My grandmother used to trap fishers with my grandfather. The animals have a beautiful dark colored fur.

Sarah pulled back her hair. "Should we be scared? Are you afraid of a fisher?"

Tess smiled. "They avoid people. Once, I was walking in the woods next to a stone wall like this one. It was raining, so the fisher didn't hear or smell me. When he turned, we stared into each other's eyes, and then a moment later he was gone."

"What does a fisher eat?" asked Sarah.

"They eat small mammals like squirrels and mice and they are one of the few animals to eat porcupines. They eat food that comes from plants, too. And every once in a long while, they kill a cat."

Sarah said, "I hope there are no fishers around my house."

They kept on following the tracks, trying to see if there might be another mystery to uncover.

46

It looked as if the fisher bounded away from the stone wall.

The trio walked by a large tree, and Jasmine looked at it. Her eyes widened. "Wow. I can see that there are five scratches on this tree, and then the marks go up the tree. What animal made these? I can't tell if the scratches are new or not."

Tess moved closer and touched the scarred tree, which had bark like dragon scales. "It might have been a fisher, because they climb trees, but the marks are too thick. It's an animal with very big claws."

Sarah took a step back. She had a guess.

Sarah said, "A bear climbed up this tree, didn't it?

She started to run. Maybe her mom had been right. The woods were dangerous.

"Come back," Tess called. "You're right. It's a bear, but it would have climbed this tree months ago to get the cherries."

Sarah took a big breath and stepped forward. She took off her mitten and placed her hands on the tree. "Some of these scratches are the size of my hand, and some are smaller. Maybe it was a mom with her cub."

Tess said, "Could be more than one cub. Bears usually have two of them every other year."

They walked around the tree and found more small claw marks.

Jasmine stopped. "There's a whole mess of tracks over there."

They hurried over. When they got near, Sarah saw big tracks, the size of her feet, with five toes.

The tracks seemed to meander every which way.

Sarah stared at the print and touched her face in disbelief. She knew there was only one animal that had such large feet. "It must be the momma bear. You said she must have left those scratch marks a long time ago."

Tess said, "See how soft the edges of the tracks are? That bear was here a day or two ago, so there's no need to worry. The only kind of bear we have in these woods is a black bear, and my grandmother called them timid bears. As long as you don't corner them, they run the other way."

Jasmine said, "How do you make sure you don't corner them? You could run into them by accident."

"If you see a bear, just walk the other way," Tess said.

Jasmine said, "I don't understand. Bears hibernate in the winter."

Sarah straightened up. "I read in a magazine that bears can wake up if they hear a loud sound. They must have heard something." She walked over to Tess. "What if they heard us?" Sarah whispered.

They started back home and picked up their speed. They passed an upturned hemlock tree. Sarah heard an unfamiliar sound. The three of them stopped to listen. It was a high-pitched chattering and then one continuous hum. They looked at one another, and Sarah got ready to jaunt again.

The sound stopped. Tess pointed with an outstretched arm to the direction they had come from, as if to say, "Hurry. Go back the way we came."

Then the chattering started again.

Tess said, "Let's go. I'll explain when we get a safe distance away."

When they had retreated, Tess said, "I think the bear's den is under that fallen tree. The sounds are newborn cubs nursing. I've never heard it before, but my grandmother told me about it."

Jamine whispered, "I wish we had an iPhone. We could have recorded the baby bears. Then our class could have heard it. I bet none of the kids have ever heard those sounds.

Sarah said, "They might even have wished they hadn't gone to Montreal."

"You'll have to come back in the spring," Tess said, "so we can take a good look at the bears' den when they're no longer using it."

Jasmine was eager to come back when the den was empty. She said, "Let's remember this spot. It's close to the stone wall."

Sarah said, "It's near a large tree that has a fork and smooth bark."

They went back the way they'd come. As they got near to Tess's house, Sarah saw her mom's car. When Tess opened the door, Sarah smelled the perfume her mom always used, and she found her sitting on the sofa.

"I thought you'd be back by now," said Sarah's mom, tapping her foot. "I sat in the car for so long that I decided to let myself in."

Tess said, "I'm so glad you made yourself at home."

"I was worried."

Sarah said walking toward her mom. "We just followed the tracks of a bear."

Her mother's face turned white. "But..."

Sarah interrupted, "We never saw the bear, but we found her den and heard the cubs making wonderful humming sounds. They were nursing."

"Really? You were safe?"

"Yes, mom," Sarah said, looking directly into her mom's face. "We were safe."

"There is probably more to this story, and I can't wait to hear it. Why don't you pack up your things and you can tell me more in the car. Say thank you and goodbye to Tess."

Sarah stared at her mom. *Why did she have to tell her to say thank you?*

Up in their bedroom, Jasmine said, "It's school in two days."

"I don't want to leave, either, but I sure miss Wind Walker."

When they went downstairs, they found Tess standing at the front door. She said, "You are welcome to come back anytime you want. Maybe we could go to the place where I found the knife, or find the bear's den. Just have your mom give me a call."

Sarah said, "I'd like to do that. We could go without snowshoes, and it would be much easier to walk."

Jasmine looked up at Tess. "Thanks so much. I would like to come back, too."

When they shut the doors of the car, Sarah's mom said, "I didn't want to spoil your adventure, but Boots is missing. He's been gone since yesterday morning."

Sarah said, "No way. I dreamed about him last night, and he seemed fine." She bit her nail. "You're wrong."

"I'd hate to even think anything happened to your cat, but I'm afraid I've heard that fishers are killing cats nearby," said Sarah's mom. "When I ran into Gladys in the supermarket, she told me a fisher had killed her cat."

She glanced in the mirror to look at the girls in the backseat. "I hate to say this. You know how much I love animals, but I wish we could kill that fisher before he kills any more cats."

Sarah furrowed her eyebrows. "Boots isn't dead. Do you even know anything about fishers?"

Her mom tightened her arms across her chest, and said, "Actually, no."

"I do," said Sarah in a loud voice. "We tracked a fisher with Tess, and she told us it has a long body and dark colored fur. They eat porcupines, not cats." Sarah continued, "If you don't know anything about a fisher, how can you know what happened?" She leaned toward her mother and put her hands on her hips. "My cat isn't dead! You can be so annoying. You think you know everything. When I went to the library with Manda, I came home late. You just about called the police, but I was late because Manda's mom went shopping at White's Market!"

Her mom reached over and stroked Sarah's leg. "I'm sorry." Sarah felt the warmth of her mom's hand, and it was comforting, but it only made her sob.

"Sweetie, I hope he is okay, but I want you to prepare yourself that he might not come home. The last time I saw Boots, he was crossing the brook, and that was yesterday. He never stays out that long. I called the animal shelter, but he wasn't there."

Chapter 13

The Dream

Sarah leaned back in her seat and tried to remember her dream. She thought it could have some clues.

She had dreamed that Boots nudged open the cat door and sniffed the soft snow in her backyard. Smelling only his own scent, he moved slowly along the snow-covered brick walkway, stretching as he walked. He passed the row of lilac bushes, and brushed against the grapevine trellis. Boots stopped at the frozen brook and lowered his head to smell the beech leaf that had just fallen from the tree. He stepped gingerly onto a snow-covered rock and jumped to the other side.

Greeted by a hillside of trees, Boots paused for a moment. Higher up on the steep slope, a snowshoe hare hopped into the shrub thicket. The hare jumped again, and her feet pushed the snow down the slope, creating little balls. As the balls rolled downhill toward Boots, they grew bigger. He pounced on one of the snowballs and tried to play, but it fell apart. He jumped onto the next one, but it, too, fell apart. Bored with the game, he scampered to the stone wall. He lowered his head, and his whiskers twitched. With his nose open wide, he smelled the snow on the wall. He wanted to make sure there were no predators, but instead he smelled the tracks of his prey. He climbed up onto a pile of flat rocks. There on the other side was a mouse eating some acorns. Boots pushed off from his white back paws, flew through the air with his black body fully stretched, and landed on the unsuspecting mouse. Since he wasn't hungry, he just nosed it, rolled it in the snow, and then continued on his way.

Chapter 14

Boots is Missing

After Sarah's mother and the two girls arrived back at Sarah's house, Sarah shoved the door open onto the back porch. She stood completely still while the cold air blew right through her.

She screamed over the sound of the wind, "Boots, Boots! Come home!" She turned in every direction and repeated the cry until she was hoarse.

Then she returned to the warmth of her house, sat down at the kitchen table, and laid her head to rest. Her tears came, and then her sobs. Jasmine sat down next to her.

A few minutes later, Sarah went to the window, watched the long shadows of the lilac bushes swaying in the stark white backyard, and shook her head in disbelief.

She looked at the full bowl of cat food next to the sink.

Just then, Gregg ran down the stairs, dressed in jeans with a light jacket, carrying his skates.

Sarah looked at him, wringing her hands. "Boots is gone. Mom thinks a fisher killed him, but I don't!"

Gregg looked at Sarah, Jasmine, and then at his mom. Grabbing a muffin and dashing out the door, he said, "Oh, you guys worry too much. I'm sure Boots isn't even missing."

Sarah went into the living room. She sighed when she passed Boots' scratching pad and his ball stuffed with catnip. When she stooped down to touch it, she saw something black and called out shrilly, "Mom, Boots is under the—Oh. It's only your ball of yarn."

Chapter 15

Searching for Boots

Sarah's mom said, "I have to go to work. Jasmine's dad told me she could stay here the rest of the day and he would pick her up after work."

After Sarah heard the garage door shut, she said, "We have to go and find Boots even though my mom would be angry. I think my dream gave me some clues as to where he is. I don't want to go alone. Will you come with me?"

Jasmine and Sarah filled their water bottles and shoved them into their backpacks. Sarah threw Jasmine some snacks to bring.

Jasmine said, "I'll bring the compass my dad gave me, just in case."

The girls grabbed their snowshoes.

"Let's get going. According to my dream, we should check the cat door," said Sarah. "Boots probably went out that way."

They put on their snowshoes that had been on the front porch and walked in the deep snow to the back of the house.

At the cat's door, they found that Boots' tracks were somewhat melted, with four toes still evident.

Jasmine measured the print by putting her hand down next to the impression. This would help her be able to identify Boots' tracks once they got into the woods.

Sarah measured it, too.

They followed the tracks passed the lilac bushes. Boots had crossed the narrowest part of the brook.

Sarah said, "I guess we'll have to jump. It doesn't

look too bad." She went as close as she could to the edge and then leaped over the partially frozen brook. The ice crackled. The middle of her snowshoe just reached the other bank.

"Glad I don't have to walk on a log again," Jasmine said. She took a leap, and landed on Boots' tracks.

Boots' prints continued, and Sarah saw several very deep impressions in a row. "I think Boots must have been jumping on some snowballs. These tracks look like he was happy."

They followed the tracks to a stone wall and climbed over it. They saw where Boots' tracks made one deep depression.

"It looks like he was going after some animal," Sarah said. "In my dream it was a mouse. Do you think he got it?"

"There's no sign of blood."

They walked on, one girl on each side of the track.

Sarah said, "It's going to be easy to follow Boots."

They traveled along the stone wall. Before long, they came to a snowmobile trail. The tracks showed that Boots had entered the trail, which circled uphill. His footprints disappeared into the packed snow.

Sarah and Jasmine stared at each other. Sarah put her mittens up to her eyes as if to hide them. "Now it'll be impossible to find Boots. It's not fair."

After a long pause, Jasmine said softly, while she moved closer to Sarah, "We can't give up. We can follow the trail uphill and look for where Boots left the path. You stay on one side of the trail, and I'll stay on the other."

Sarah mumbled, "Maybe that will work," and dried her tears. "We should keep on looking until we find a good track. And if we don't find Boots, maybe someone snow-mobiling saw him.""

They bent their heads as they walked on the crunchy snow.

Jasmine stopped. "Come here."

Sarah looked at the tracks. "I can barely make it out. This track may have four or five toes."

The prints were not in a line. There were two tracks, a space, and then two more.

"This one has one, two, three, four, five toes," Sarah said. "Oh, no! It can't be. It looks like what we saw with Tess. It's a fisher."

Jasmine knelt down beside her. "I'm sorry."

"Don't be sorry," Sarah said, and stared back at Jasmine. "We need more evidence to know what happened."

Jasmine said. "I don't see any drag marks, but if your cat is small the fisher could've had him in its mouth."

"Don't say that."

Jasmine unfolded her arms and followed the tracks. Sarah imagined the fisher moving like an accordion, with Boots in its mouth. She wanted to walk slowly, because she was so afraid of what she might find, but she moved quickly. There was a chance that Boots was still alive. The tracks showed that the fisher had continued bounding. Off in the distance, Sarah saw a huge rock outcropping. The girls moved uphill through the forest. The tracks of the fisher were now in a straight line, with small spaces between steps; the animal had slowed down. They sensed something lay ahead of them. Beech saplings with dried leaves blocked their view. The tracks seemed to head straight for the biggest boulder.

As they approached, Jasmine said, "Look at the rock. There's a hole.... Something's next to it, and it's very bloody."

They couldn't make it out. As they got closer, they saw the remains of an animal, with only its head left. Sarah froze. Her tears flowed like a waterfall. She slumped to the ground. Then she noticed tiny pointed sticks next to her.

Sarah lifted a fisted hand to the sky. She said, "It's not Boots. Those are quills. It's a dead porcupine."

She pushed herself up. The she reached toward Jasmine and took her hand.

"You're right," Jasmine said, tightening the squeeze. "Let's get out of here and go back to the snowmobile trail to find Boots, before it's too late."

Chapter 16

The Search Continues

On the packed trail, they continued to scan the ground for Boots' tracks. They picked up their pace. They had stayed out longer than they had expected. Sarah's stomach growled, but she paid it no mind.

She waved her arm rapidly and called to Jasmine, "Boots' tracks! Come here!"

Each print looked like a circle containing the impressions of the pad and the four toes. There were no claw marks.

Without speaking, they swiftly pursued the prints, until they came to a red oak tree covered with snow.

Sarah said with glee, "The tracks go up and then down the other side. It's Boots."

She started running, tripped over her snowshoe, and fell. She pushed herself over to a small tree, grabbed on to it, and pulled herself up.

"Are you all right?" Jasmine asked.

"Yup," Sarah replied, and brushed off the snow.

After they'd walked a few more yards, Jasmine said, "Do you see that track next to the tree? There's melted snow, too." She stooped down to take a closer look. "I'm sure it's pee."

Sarah wondered why Jasmine had a frown.

"Dogs pee off to the side of the trail," said Jasmine, "not cats. It's got to be a dog—or maybe a fox. We should go back to the snowmobile trail."

"It can't be a fox. They don't climb trees."

Jasmine said, shaking her head, "It's not a cat. It's not Boots."

"I want to keep going," Sarah said in a loud gruff voice. "You're wrong!"

Jasmine took a deep breath. "It can't be Boots. Ever see him lift his leg to pee?"

"No."

"Let's go back," Jasmine said.

Sarah looked at the tree and then at the tracks. *It just had to be Boots. But what if Jasmine was right?* "I still think you're wrong. I want to find Boots. Are you coming with me?"

To stop the argument, Jasmine quickly spun around to face Sarah. She lost her balance and fell right into a broken spruce branch.

"Ow!"

She put her hand to her face, and looked at her mitten.

"I'm bleeding."

Sarah moved closer and saw a puncture in Jasmine's cheek, right next to her eye. *Oh, no*, she thought, *we'll have to go back. I guess we won't be able to find Boots.*

Aloud Sarah said, "Don't worry. I know what to do." She reached down and picked up some snow. "Use this to clean your cut off and then press on it. Maybe you can stop the bleeding. When I fell biking and ripped my pants, my dad told me to press on the cut."

"It hurts a little," Jasmine said through gritted teeth. Then she dropped the snow and pulled out the mirrored compass from her pocket. "It looks terrible."

She scooped up some more snow and cleaned the pieces of bark off her face, but the wound remained.

Sarah bit her lip. *Could Jasmine still search? Maybe the cut wasn't that bad.* Then Sarah looked and saw that blood was dripping from the cut. She stroked Jasmine's shoulder. "Let's go home. You might need stitches, or it might get infected."

"I'll be all right. We've come so far. Let's go to the trail and look some more."

Chapter 17

Hot on Boots' Track

Back on the snowmobile trail, Jasmine and Sarah continued to track.

Sarah caught up to Jasmine. "I know you don't want to stop. I don't either, but your cut looks deep."

Jasmine paused. She bent her head down, and stared at the ground. As the sun emerged from behind a cloud, the snow glistened. Jasmine knelt down and rubbed her hand on the snow. "Come here. In this light, I can see a print. Could be Boots' track going back to your house."

"You found it!" Sarah said punching her fist into the air.

Sarah looked around and found another faint track. When the sun clouded over again, she followed the prints slowly because they were harder to see.

"I found a clear print," Sarah said after a few moments, and she bent down over a log without much snow that showed four toe marks. "It has nails, and it was circling this big piece of wood."

Jasmine lowered her head. "It's a dog. Look, there's a blue house over there. Maybe that's its home. The tracks are coming and going from that direction."

Sarah said, looking at the house, "You're right. It's not Boots." With a big sigh, she sat down on a rock. "We're never going to find him. I guess we should go home." She called out to Boots one more time in each direction, the way Tess had done with the owl. When she looked up, she saw something speckled halfway up the tree. She wondered what could look like that. To get a better view, she got up and shifted her body back and forth. *Could it be a bobcat, like the one that had killed the fawn?* The animal in the tree had the same coloring she had seen in her book.

Sarah walked closer and still couldn't make it out. Then she heard "Meow."

Sarah shouted, "You're alive! You're alive!"

Jasmine said, "He's safe!"

In the fork of the tree sat Boots, camouflaged by the pine needles, except for his white paws.

"Come down," Sarah cried. She looked back at the tracks leading to the blue house, and then at Boots. "That dumb dog must have chased you up this tree."

Jasmine said, "Cats climb up trees—not down them."

"This happened to Boots before," said Sarah. "Gregg went on the Internet to figure out what to do. It said to place a ladder against the tree, so we tried it, and he climbed down."

"We don't have a ladder, but the pine tree has branches that circle it," said Jasmine.

Sarah and Jasmine strained their necks upward and talked calmly to Boots. He didn't move.

"Meow, meow, meow."

"Boots, it's me. You're safe. Come down from the tree!"

"Meoooow, meoooow."

The cat just sat still where the branches formed a V.

Sarah said, "I'm worried. I can barely see him, and he looks all scrunched up. He sure is nervous. Oh, wait—I brought Boots' special treats. Maybe he'll smell them."

Sarah pulled off her mittens, opened the bag, and managed to pull out some food with her frozen hand. Then Jasmine and Sarah walked back and forth and called out, "Boots, come here."

He inched down backward, first with his back white paws and then with his front ones.

Sarah raised her voice, lifting her chin. "Boots, you can do it."

While he clung to the tree, a big white dog with brown ears bounded toward them.

Boots scurried at top speed to an even higher branch than before.

"Get out of here," Sarah shouted at the dog, and waved her hand. "Go!"

She looked up again, and called, "Boots. Boots, come down."

Boots stayed where he was.

Sarah said, "We must get this stupid dog out of here."

The dog kept barking.

"Boots is probably frozen. I'm giving some of Boots' food to the dog to shut him up," said Sarah.

"Yeah. Try it."

"Meow, meow."

Sarah threw some of Boots' treats onto the snow. The dog came toward the colored squares, but kept on barking. Suddenly, its ears perked up, and the girls heard a faint whistle three times.

After a few more barks, the dog bounded toward the house.

"Meow, meow."

"Boots, the dog is gone," Sarah said. "It's safe."

They called out to Boots. Sarah pulled her hair back. *What if something happens if he tries to climb down?* she thought.

"He's not moving," said Jasmine. "I'm going to that blue house to get help."

"No. He's freezing. I've got to get him down right now. I can climb up the tree. It's perfect. The first branch isn't that high. Please give me a lift."

Jasmine said, "It's not safe."

"I know I can do it. Remember the brook. If I say I can, I can."

Sarah bent down and undid her snowshoe bindings. "Just give me a little lift." Jasmine cupped her hands to make a step.

Sarah placed her boot in Jasmine's hands, reached for the biggest branch, and tried to pull herself up. Her mitten fell off. She looked down at the ground.

"I'll have to keep climbing without it."

She tried again, but the wet branch was slippery. Finally, Sarah grabbed the bough firmly, pulled her body above the limb, and swung her leg up and over. She stood up leaning on the trunk of the tree. Snow showered from the limb above. She felt dizzy. Remembering she needed to gaze at one point to get back her balance, she scanned the forest, found a hole in a nearby sugar maple, and stared at it.

"Meow."

Sarah stretched out her arm, and then her whole body, grabbed a higher branch, and stepped onto the next limb, using the trunk of the tree for support. Every muscle of her face tightened as she concentrated.

"Meooow, meooow."

Sarah looked at the next big limb. She tried several times to reach it, but she could touch it only by standing on her tiptoes. Sarah couldn't get hold of it. She yelled, "It's impossible. It's too high." She looked at Boots hidden by the needles. "Boots, I can't do it!"

Sarah leaned her head against the tree and felt tears pouring down her cheeks. Her whole body started to shake. She put her hands around the tree and held it tightly.

Boots didn't move.

Jasmine called up. "Come down, Sarah."

Sarah didn't answer. Still crying, she stretched out her arms toward her cat.

"Meoooow, meoooow."

Suddenly, Jasmine called out, "He's coming down. He's gripping the tree with all his claws."

Sarah looked up. "I can't see him."

"Meow."

"Boots, Boots, you can do it," Sarah said. She wiped her tears so she could see.

"Meow, meow."

Boots jumped to a thin dead limb.

Sarah cried out, "Be careful."

She shifted her body so she could see him better. The thick pine needles blocked her vision.

"I can't see him anymore," called Sarah.

"Neither can I."

Tears started pouring down Sarah's face again. The wind picked up, and the snow swirled around her. She leaned her head back to squint through the flurry of snow-flakes. She saw only white. She tried wiping the snow from her eyes.

A moment later, Sarah said, "Ouch."

She felt nails in her neck and heard her jacket rip. Then she smiled and leaned against the tree. "You made it. You heard me crying. You're the most wonderful cat in the world."

Jasmine called up, "Yes!"

Boots licked Sarah's face, and she stroked him with one hand.

"Purr, purr."

The wind picked up, and Jasmine called out, "Be careful. It's getting dark."

"Boots, we have to get you down the rest of the way before I lose my balance. But I can't with you on my shoulder." She didn't know what to do.

Boots did. He leaped from her shoulder and landed on the ground on all fours, sinking into the snow.

Sarah stepped down to the limb below, and then jumped, calling out, "I'm coming!"

She hit the snow and ran to Boots. She picked him up, cuddled him just as they always did before she went to sleep. "Are you okay?"

"I bet he needs some water," Jasmine said. "I have this bottle of water, but I can't think of anything to put it in. I have an idea." She bent down and pressed the snow to make a bowl. She unwrapped two granola bars and used the aluminum foil to line the snow bowl. Jasmine poured in the water. Boots lapped it up, and his panting slowed down.

Sarah beamed as she bent down to pet Boots.

Then Jasmine looked at her wound in her compass mirror, and smiled when she saw the bleeding had stopped.

After he had finished drinking the water, Boots lowered his nose to smell the ground, and took off toward home.

Jasmine started to follow him, while Sarah grabbed her snowshoes and put them on.

When Boots reached the snowmobile trail, he picked up his pace.

Sarah said, "Oh, no. He'd better be going home. I don't want to lose him again."

At the stone wall, Sarah looked down. "Boots' tracks. They're going down toward the brook."

"I see it, too."

The girls practically slid down the hill. They reached the brook in time to see Boots passing the lilacs and entering the cat door.

Sarah and Jasmine hugged each other and jumped up and down as best they could in snowshoes. Sarah said, "I can't believe we did it. Let's call Tess and tell her what happened."

Jasmine squeezed Sarah's hand.

Sarah opened the front door and found her mom by the fire, kneeling and petting Boots.

"Purr, purr."

"Where you have been? I've been sick with worry."

Sarah didn't answer. She swooped down, picked Boots up, and held him on her shoulder.

"Purr, purr."

Boots walked down Sarah's back and headed to the kitchen. He was lapping up the water just as Gregg walked down the stairs to get a snack from the refrigerator.

With soda in hand, he came into the living room and stared at the three of them. "You all worry too much. Boots is in the kitchen; he's probably been hiding in the house for the last day or so. What was all the fuss? He looks just fine."

Later that night, Boots snuggled with Sarah. She said, "I have two questions. First, I wonder what animal acted like both a dog and a cat." She remembered that Jasmine thought it might be some kind of fox, so she went on the Internet and searched for the words "fox climb trees." The first hit was http://www.bear-tracker.com/grayfox.html. The website showed pictures of a gray fox climbing a tree, and tracks that looked round.

The second question she wouldn't know the answer to until tomorrow.

Chapter 18

Back at the Stable

In the morning, Sarah jerked up, looking for Boots. She smiled when she saw him curled up at the end of her bed.

Sarah stroked him. "You'd better stay in the house while I'm gone. Wish me good luck. I'm going to try to jump Walker." She bit her lip.

Boots jumped off the bed and scampered down the stairs.

Sarah texted Jasmine, "I jump W. Can you come?"

"9?"

"Yes."

The snow was blowing hard when Sarah, dressed up in riding clothes, arrived at the stable. She could hardly see through the snow and almost bumped into Lucy.

"You're back,'" Lucy said. "How was your tracking adventure?"

"It was worth it. Jasmine and I rescued Boots."

Before Lucy could ask any more questions, Sarah flew to the barn to find Walker.

He was in the stable eating fresh hay, which smelled sweet. Sarah looked down at Walker's leg. The bandage was gone. She patted him. "*Maybe it wasn't so bad after all.*"

Jasmine walked into the barn. Sarah said, "Walker's leg looks healed and has a good scab. What do you think?"

Jasmine bent down on one knee. "Seems okay to me."

Jasmine went for the saddle.

Sarah got on a stool, placed the saddle on Walker's back, and cinched it. She led him to the arena and around the ring several times, checking to see if he was in good spirits. When she stopped, he did, too. When she led him to the left, he followed. He responded to her every move. Sarah knew they were both ready. She mounted him and took several deep breaths. After circling a few times, Sarah said to Walker, "I can feel it now. I feel how you shift from side to side."

When she had him trot, she held her head straight ahead. She checked if Walker's ears were relaxed.

Lucy said, "Try to trot with Walker with your eyes closed."

Sarah swayed with Walker. When she opened her eyes, she smiled. It was time to jump.

Sarah said, "Jasmine, would you put the jumping bar to twenty four inches. I know I can do that much today."

As Sarah got close to the fence, she felt her breath match Walker's. His front feet lifted off the ground, his back arched, and then one at a time, his feet touched down.

Sarah stroked Walker. "Good jumping."

Lucy called out, "That's good, but your shoulders aren't level, and don't lean so far forward."

Sarah shifted her body and straightened her back.

Lucy said, "Try again."

She circled Walker around. She whispered, "We can do it."

He started cantering toward the bar, and they flew over the fence.

Lucy called out, "That was terrific. You were at just the right angle. Try it again, and see if you can repeat it." She did.

Sarah said, "Can you raise the bar to thirty inches?"

"Hon, that's pushing it," Lucy said. "You've done better than you ever have before. Wait until another day."

"Please. I dreamed of doing this the whole time I was tracking."

Lucy shifted back and forth. "Are you sure you want to do it?"

"I helped Jasmine and Tess cross a brook. I feel like I do when I'm dancing and nothing else matters."

Jasmine said, "I know she can do it."

Lucy looked at Jasmine, who was smiling. "Okay. Go ahead."

Sarah stared straight ahead, took a deep breath, and cantered Walker around the ring. Lucy called out, "Think like Walker."

Sarah hoped she wouldn't think at all—just feel him.

Sarah looked at the bar and noticed that Manda and Rachael had entered the arena. Her heart beat a little faster, but surprisingly, they yelled, "Good luck."

With that encouragement, Sarah headed toward the bar. As she neared it, Walkers front legs lifted up, and they soared through the air. Then, one at a time, Walker's feet landed solidly.

Sarah caressed him. "We did it."

When Sarah dismounted, Lucy, Jasmine, Manda, and Rachael encircled her and cheered. Sarah cheered, too. Jasmine hugged her.

When Sarah caught her breath, she and Wind Walker strolled back to the barn, chatting with Jasmine. The falling snow enveloped the three of them, but Sarah's smile was no secret.

About the Author

PHOTO © ANTHONY RECZEK

In addition to *Snow Secrets*, Lynn Levine has co-authored two books: *Mammal Tracks and Scat: Life Size-Tracking Guide* and *Working with Your Woodland: A Landowner's Guide*.

Lynn was born in Brooklyn and moved to Vermont in 1974. Four years later, having received her master's degree in forestry from the University of Massachusetts, Lynn became the first female consulting forester in New England. Throughout her career, she has been passionate about protecting the integrity of the forest.

Lynn has inspired young people and adults to connect with the woods. She has taken thousands of people into the forest to share her love of nature, and to spur others to feel the same. She has found that teaching tracking is one powerful way to spark and enhance that bond.

A group of 4th graders anointed Lynn "*The Scat Lady*"—a quirky title she cherishes.

You can find more information about her programs and her books at her website www.heartwoodpress.com.

Lynn lives in the woods of Dummerston, Vermont with her husband.